Collins

English in 5 minutes

Grammar, punctuation and spelling activities

Jon Goulding

CONTENTS

HOW TO USE THIS BOOK

The best way to help your child to build their confidence in English grammar, punctuation and spelling is to give them lots and lots of practice in the key topics and skills.

Written by English experts, this series will help your child master English grammar, punctuation and spelling, and prepare them for SATs.

This book provides ready-to-practise questions that comprehensively cover the English grammar, punctuation and spelling curriculum for Year 3. It contains:

- 36 topic-based tests, each 5 minutes long, to help your child build up their grammar, punctuation and spelling knowledge day-by-day.

- 4 mixed topic tests (Progress Tests), each 5 minutes long, to check progress by covering a mix of topics from the previous 9 tests.

Each test is divided into three Steps:

- **Step 1: Review (1 minute)**
  This exercise helps your child to revise grammar, punctuation and spelling topics they should already know and prepares them for Step 2.

- **Step 2: Practise (2½ minutes)**
  This exercise is a set of questions focused on the topic area being tested.

- **Step 3: Challenge (1½ minutes)**
  This is a more testing exercise designed to stretch your child and deepen their understanding.

Some of the tests also include a Tip to help your child answer questions of a particular type.

Your child should attempt to answer as many questions as possible in the time allowed at each Step. Answers are provided at the back of the book.

To help to measure progress, each test includes boxes for recording the date of the test, the total score obtained, and the total time taken. One mark is awarded for each written part of the answer.

Acknowledgements

The authors and publisher are grateful to the copyright holders for permission to use quoted materials and images.

All images are © HarperCollins*Publishers* Ltd and © Shutterstock.com

Every effort has been made to trace copyright holders and obtain their permission for the use of copyright material. The authors and publisher will gladly receive information enabling them to rectify any error or omission in subsequent editions. All facts are correct at time of going to press.

Published by Collins
An imprint of HarperCollins*Publishers*
1 London Bridge Street
London SE1 9GF

HarperCollins*Publishers*
1st Floor, Watermarque Building,
Ringsend Road, Dublin 4, Ireland

ISBN: 978-0-00-844942-1

First published 2021

10 9 8 7 6 5 4 3 2 1

British Library Cataloguing in Publication Data.

A CIP record of this book is available from the British Library.

Author: Jon Goulding
Publisher: Fiona McGlade
Project Manager: Chantal Addy
Editor: Jill Laidlaw
Cover Design: Kevin Robbins and Sarah Duxbury
Inside Concept Design: Paul Oates and Ian Wrigley
Typesetting Services: Jouve India Private Limited
Production: Karen Nulty
Printed in Great Britain by Martins the Printers

Nouns and expanded noun phrases

Date: 23/12/2022

Day of week: Friday

> **Tip** Remember, a **noun** is the name of a thing, person or place. An **expanded noun phrase** contains a noun and additional words to describe the noun, for example, 'the *friendly, small* kitten'.

STEP 1 (1 min) Review

Select the most suitable **adjective** to describe the underlined **noun** in each noun phrase.

tall	fast	loud	slow

the _loud_ thunder

my _slow_ snail

a _fast_ train

the _tall_ tower

STEP 2 (2.5 min) Practise

Insert **two adjectives** before each **noun** then draw a line to match the start of each sentence to the most suitable **expanded noun phrase**.

Sam was running on   the _small, big_ painting.

Dad paid   the _ginger, scary_ cat.

Martha looked at   the _stunning, green_ field.

Brewster barked at   the _brave, strong_ taxi driver.

STEP 3 (1.5 min) Challenge

Write a sentence which includes an **expanded noun phrase** for each picture.

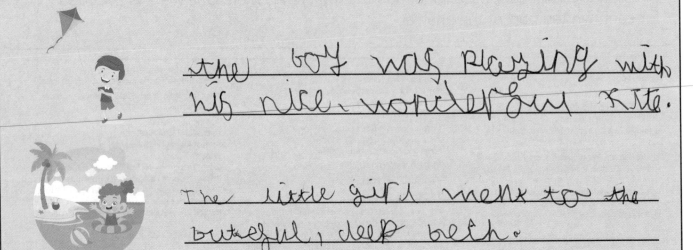

the boy was playing with his nice, wonderful kite.

The little girl went to the beautiful, deep beach.

Time spent: ___ min ___ sec. Total: ___ out of 18

©HarperCollinsPublishers 2021

Adjectives and adverbs

Tip *An adjective can describe a noun. An adverb can be used to give more information about a verb, for example, 'She ran **quickly**.' The adverb **quickly** describes how she ran.*

STEP 1 (1 min) Review

Write the most suitable **adverb** in each sentence. Use each word once.

silently	carefully	slowly	greedily

The snow melted ___slowly___ over several days.

He ___carefully___ cut the wood with the sharp saw.

My horse ___greedily___ gobbled the carrots.

We crept ___silently___ through the dark corridors.

STEP 2 (2.5 min) Practise

Change the words in bold to **adverbs** and **adjectives** that make sense.

We all played **happy** in the **amazingly** treehouse.

[   ] [   ]

Incredible, Ali's horse jumped over the **hugely** fences.

[   ]   [   ]

They walked **weary** towards the **cosily** shelter.

[   ]   [   ]

STEP 3 (1.5 min) Challenge

Read the short passage below. Underline the **adjectives** and circle the **adverbs**.

As the amazing rocket flew rapidly towards the huge, red planet, Charlie slept restlessly. He dreamed of scary aliens angrily chasing him. As he woke, he slowly realised it had been a silly dream. He dressed quickly and went back to the controls of the mighty spaceship.

Tip *Coordinating conjunctions can be used to join two words, phrases or clauses to make one sentence. Subordinating conjunctions introduce a subordinate clause, linking it to a main clause. The subordinate clause does not make sense on its own.*

STEP 1 ⏱ 1 min **Review**

Add the correct **conjunction** to each sentence. Use each only once.

or	when	but	because

They rushed to the shop _____ it was closed.

We ate fruit _____ we were hungry.

I wore my hat _____ it was cold.

Nav does not like chocolate _____ crisps.

STEP 2 ⏱ 2.5 min **Practise**

Rewrite each pair of sentences joining the two parts with a suitable **conjunction**.

They had ice cold water. They were hot.

_____

It was a long journey. The car was uncomfortable.

_____

STEP 3 ⏱ 1.5 min **Challenge**

For each sentence below, write the **conjunction**. Then write **C** for **coordinating** or **S** for **subordinating**.

Milly can play tennis and she is a really good player. _____ ___

We will miss the bus if we walk slowly. _____ ___

You can draw a picture or you can make a model. _____ ___

Time spent: _____ min _____ sec. Total: _____ out of 12

Date: _____

Day of week: _____

 Tip *Conjunctions can be used to show **why** something happens (cause). They can also link a cause with an effect (what happens), for example, 'It was raining **so** they stayed inside.'*

STEP 1 (1 min) Review

Choose the correct **conjunction** to complete each sentence.

We need a towel _____ we are going swimming. **because / but**

I want to be a good swimmer _____ I can go to the deep end. **when / so**

There will be no swimming _____ we are silly. **so / if**

We wear goggles _____ we swim underwater. **but / when**

STEP 2 (2.5 min) Practise

Place a tick next to each example where the **conjunction** is used to join the cause and the effect parts of a sentence together.

Lou is brilliant at dancing and really good at writing. ☐

Java eats lots of fruit because it is healthy. ☐

You can use the pen but you must return it. ☐

Nature will water the garden if it rains. ☐

STEP 3 (1.5 min) Challenge

Write **three** sentences. Start each sentence with the effect, then write a **conjunction**, then add the **cause**.

effect – *snow in the garden melts* 		cause – *warm day*

_____

effect – *the twins were excited* 		cause – *it was their birthday*

_____

effect – *we can go outside* 		cause – *finishing our lunch*

_____

5 | Conjunctions (time)

Date: _____

Day of week: _____

Tip *Conjunctions can also be used to show **when** something happens (time).*

STEP 1 (1 min) Review

Complete each sentence with a **conjunction** that shows *time*.

when	before	after	while

You can come to my house _____ we have played football.

Go to the toilet _____ we get on the bus.

I will make the meal _____ you set the table.

You will see Buckingham Palace _____ you go to London.

STEP 2 (2.5 min) Practise

Match each sentence starter to the event that happens, adding the correct **conjunction** to indicate *time*.

They were all throwing snowballs _____   it broke down.

We could not use the car _____   the thunderstorm raged.

Lucy was asleep _____   it is the summer holidays.

They always go camping _____   their hands got so cold.

STEP 3 (1.5 min) Challenge

For each picture, write a sentence containing the given **conjunction**.

 **before**

_____

_____

 **when**

_____

_____

Time spent: _____ min _____ sec. Total: _____ out of 14

Date: _____

Day of week: _____

Tip *Adverbs can be used in sentences to describe when (time), where (place) and why (cause).*

STEP 1 (1 min) Review

Write each **adverb** in the correct sentence.

soon	through	therefore	since

She hasn't visited the village _____ last year. **time**

The hole in the roof let lots of water _____. **place**

The car would not start _____ they walked. **cause**

We will pedal fast to make sure we get there _____. **time**

STEP 2 (2.5 min) Practise

Replace each word or phrase in bold with a **single adverb**. Label each adverb *time*, *place* or *cause*.

The train was going slowly but they knew they would arrive **in the end**.

_____ _____

She had to eat the vegetables **or** she would get no dessert.

_____ _____

There were trees **in each direction** they looked.

_____ _____

STEP 3 (1.5 min) Challenge

Write a sentence containing each given **adverb**.

afterwards

_____

_____

consequently

_____

_____

Tip *Prepositions are used to explain **where** something is (place) or **when** something is happening (time).*

STEP 1 (1 min) Review

Underline the **preposition** in each sentence and write **P** if it is being used for **place** and **T** if it is being used for **time**.

They huddled together next to the warm fire. _____

The bear rested in the shade. _____

We went shopping after school. _____

A large wasp landed on the apple. _____

STEP 2 (2.5 min) Practise

Write a sentence containing a suitable **preposition** for each picture.

place _____

_____

_____

time _____

_____

_____

STEP 3 (1.5 min) Challenge

Rewrite the passage below, replacing the incorrect **prepositions** with the correct ones.

They had PE during Monday. They all loved being through the school gym. They had to walk in the playground to get there. There was always time for a game on the lesson.

_____

_____

_____

10

Time spent: _____ min _____ sec. Total: _____ out of 14

©HarperCollins*Publishers* 2021

Date: _____

Day of week: _____

Tip *Tense refers to when we are talking about something which has already happened (past) or something happening now (present). The form of the verb changes depending on the tense. For example, 'we rode' (simple past tense), 'we ride' (simple present tense), 'we were riding' (past progressive tense) and 'we are riding' (present progressive tense).*

STEP 1 (1 min) **Review**

Use the correct form of the **verb** so that each sentence is in the **simple past** tense.

We _____ a lovely meal.   **eat**

The plane _____ low over our heads.   **fly**

Everyone _____ well together.   **play**

Sally _____ the ball very hard.   **kick**

STEP 2 (2.5 min) **Practise**

Underline the **two words** in each sentence which show the **past progressive** or **present progressive** tense. Write **past** or **present** after each sentence.

The birds were flying south for the winter.   _____

The children are swimming in the sea.   _____

A cold wind is blowing from the east.   _____

Tigger the cat was purring on the cushion.   _____

STEP 3 (1.5 min) **Challenge**

Read the passage and identify the incorrect verbs. Write the **two correct words** in each box to show that events were ongoing. The first one has been done for you.

The submarines was dived under the sea. One by one they disappeared. The fastest

┌─────────────────────┐
│   **were diving**   │
└─────────────────────┘

were led the race. Josh were stand on the shore. He were thought how boring

┌──────────────┐ ┌──────────────┐   ┌──────────────┐
│   │ │   │   │   │
└──────────────┘ └──────────────┘   └──────────────┘

submarine races are to watch.

 **Tip** *The present perfect tense is used to talk about completed events that have happened before now (the present). The present tense of the verb 'to have' is used with the past participle of the main verb – for example, 'we have ridden'.*

STEP 1 (1 min) **Review**

Complete each sentence with '**has**' or '**have**' to ensure the sentences make sense in the **present perfect** tense.

The children _____ gone to school.

A large ship _____ sailed into the harbour.

Dad _____ made an amazing cake.

We _____ walked here.

STEP 2 (2.5 min) **Practise**

Write both the **main verb** and the verb '**to have**' in the correct form to complete each sentence in the **present perfect** tense.

They _____ _____ in a talent show. (**perform**)

Emile _____ _____ all his homework. (**complete**)

My sister _____ _____ to school. (**walk**)

The teachers _____ _____ to us about being kind. (**talk**)

STEP 3 (1.5 min) **Challenge**

Write a brief explanation of why the sentence below is **not** in the **present perfect** tense. What needs to change?

The hare and the tortoise has racing each other.

_____

_____

Time spent: _____ min _____ sec. Total: _____ out of 14

Date: _____

Day of week: _____

STEP 1 (1 min) **Review**

- Write the words below in the correct place in the table.

so	when	after	because	if	while

Conjunctions showing cause	Conjunctions showing time

STEP 2 (2.5 min) **Practise**

- Choose a suitable **preposition** to add to each sentence.

We sat and ate popcorn _____ the film.   (time)

The cat jumped _____ the dog.   (place)

Amy hid her diary _____ her bed.   (place)

We have to get out of the forest _____ dark.   (time)

STEP 3 (1.5 min) **Challenge**

- Rewrite each sentence in the given **tense**.

The children ran in a race.

past progressive _____ .

Everyone plays in the stream before they walk home.

simple past _____

The whole class is walking to the swimming baths.

present perfect _____

11 Using 'a' or 'an'

> **Tip** When using 'a' or 'an' before a noun or adjective, it is important to know whether the first letter of the noun or adjective has a vowel sound or a consonant sound. If the noun or adjective has a vowel sound, use 'an' before it, for example, **an apple**. If the noun or adjective has a consonant sound, use 'a' before it, for example, **a bike**. The letters **a, e, i, o** and **u** are vowels and all the other letters of the alphabet are consonants.

STEP 1 (1 min) Review

Complete each sentence with 'a' or 'an'.

We found _____ secret path at the end of the garden.

Under the moonlight they could see _____ eerie shape.

Zak was lost so he asked _____ old man for directions.

We had to buy _____ new tent after the storm.

STEP 2 (2.5 min) Practise

Add a suitable **adjective** to each sentence.

From the mountain top, they could see an _____ view.

All the children wanted to play on an _____ swing in the garden.

The birthday cake was in the shape of a _____ car.

Everybody laughed when she told a _____ joke.

STEP 3 (1.5 min) Challenge

Underline the incorrect use of 'a' and 'an' in the sentences below.

We had a early lunch and went on a adventure in an big boat. A huge whale passed by and we saw a octopus and an old shipwreck.

Explain why 'a apple' and 'an melon' are incorrect.

_____

_____

Time spent: _____ min _____ sec. Total: _____ out of 14

Date: _____

Day of week: _____

Tip

Capital letters are used for names of people and places (such as countries, towns, cities, oceans and rivers). Days of the week and months of the year also need capital letters.

STEP 1 (1 min) Review

Circle each of the words which should have a **capital letter**.

edward	forest	italy	tuesday	chicken	beach
city	jupiter	slowly	april	countryside	lucy

STEP 2 (2.5 min) Practise

Copy the following sentence, adding **capital letters** where needed.

every wednesday during the month of february, mrs jones will swim with crocodiles in the river nile near the city of cairo in egypt.

_____

_____

_____

STEP 3 (1.5 min) Challenge

Explain why the words '**ocean**' and '**river**' should not have a **capital letter**, but '**River Thames**' and '**Pacific Ocean**' do have **capital letters**.

_____

_____

Explain the difference between '**March**' and '**march**' if these words appeared in the middle of sentences.

_____

_____

Date: _____

Day of week: _____

STEP 1 (1 min) Review

Which sentence is **punctuated correctly**?

It was a lovely day when Harry went surfing ☐

it was a lovely day when Harry went surfing. ☐

It was a lovely day when Harry went surfing. ☐

It was a lovely day when harry went surfing. ☐

STEP 2 (2.5 min) Practise

Explain what is wrong with the **punctuation** of the sentence below.

we visited the theatre yesterday and saw an amazing play

_____

_____

STEP 3 (1.5 min) Challenge

Copy the following text, adding the missing **capital letters** and **full stops** to make **three** separate sentences.

the divers were fascinated by the shark it was gliding silently through the water like a sleek, grey submarine beneath their boat when it was close enough, martha took a photograph

_____

_____

_____

Time spent: _____ min _____ sec. Total: _____ out of 10

Date: _____

Day of week: _____

Tip Question marks are used at the end of a question sentence. Exclamation marks are used at the end of exclamation sentences when something is being emphasised or to show surprise.

STEP 1 (1 min) Review

Which sentence uses an **exclamation mark** correctly?

What an incredible view we saw! ☐   Is your name is Jess! ☐   What time is it! ☐

Which sentence uses a **question mark** correctly?

How beautiful the flowers are? ☐   Everybody is dancing? ☐   Is it time to leave? ☐

STEP 2 (2.5 min) Practise

Add the correct **punctuation mark** to each sentence.

What a huge beanstalk Jack saw before him____

Where could it have come from____

How would he climb it____

How terrifying the giant was____

STEP 3 (1.5 min) Challenge

Copy the following text, making sure the correct **punctuation** is used throughout.

During the day, the creature sleeps but at night it stirs in its cave? It sees well in the dark as it creeps through the forest! Munch. It snatches a small mammal from a tree branch. What could it be! What else does it eat! How incredible this creature is.

_____

_____

_____

Date: _____

Day of week: _____

Tip *Commas can be used to separate items in a list.*

STEP 1 (1 min) Review

Place the **commas** in the correct places in each sentence below.

We saw elephants lions giraffes and baboons when we went to the zoo.

They visited the cities of London Manchester Birmingham and Leeds on their holiday.

STEP 2 (2.5 min) Practise

Which sentence below uses **commas** correctly?

Hetty could play, the guitar the violin the cello and, the piano. ☐

Hetty could play, the guitar the violin, the cello, and the piano ☐

Hetty could play, the guitar, the violin, the cello and the piano. ☐

Hetty could play the guitar, the violin, the cello and the piano. ☐

STEP 3 (1.5 min) Challenge

Write a sentence which lists **four** items that Dad bought at the supermarket.

_____

_____

Write a sentence which includes a list of **four** things that Mum would like to do at the beach.

_____

_____

Time spent: _____ min _____ sec. Total: _____ out of 7

Date: _____

Day of week: _____

Tip When we write the exact words spoken by a person in a story or other text, it is known as *direct speech. This is punctuated with inverted commas (also known as speech marks) which are placed around the exact words being spoken. For example, "Let's play in the sand," said Arthur.*

STEP 1 (1 min) Review

Underline the exact words that are spoken in each sentence.

Go and get your uniform on said Mum.

This is the best food I've ever tasted said Jack.

Dad asked is this the correct train for York?

What fantastic acting that was exclaimed Cally.

STEP 2 (2.5 min) Practise

Which **two** sentences have the **inverted commas** in the correct place?

"Come into the water, shouted Ellie." ☐

It is really quite warm, "called Alex." ☐

"It's absolutely freezing!" screamed Netty. ☐

Gran said, "I think you were tricked, Netty." ☐

STEP 3 (1.5 min) Challenge

Add **inverted commas** in the correct places in the following text.

Shark! Shark! yelled Dan.

Gran shouted, Get out of the water! Quick!

It's ok Gran, laughed Netty.

Dan has a dog called Shark, explained Alex.

Date: _____

Day of week: _____

Tip Sometimes, two words can be pushed together to make a single, shorter word. For example, 'do not' can be shortened to 'don't' and 'I am' can be shortened to 'I'm'. This is called contraction. A punctuation mark known as an **apostrophe** is used in place of the missing letters.

STEP 1 (1 min) Review

Draw lines to match each **contraction** to the words written in their full form.

I am   you are   he is   could not   will not   did not

he's   didn't   I'm   won't   you're   couldn't

STEP 2 (2.5 min) Practise

Read the text below. In the boxes, write the full forms of the **contracted words**.

We're going on a school trip to a castle. It'll take three hours to get there but we don't

[_____]   [_____]   [_____]

mind going on a long journey as we haven't been on a trip for ages. The teachers

[_____]

have said they'll buy us an ice cream if they're not disturbed on the coach.

[_____]   [_____]

Mrs Williams says she's going to sleep all the way.

[_____]

STEP 3 (1.5 min) Challenge

Rewrite the following passage. Change each pair of words in bold to the correct **contraction**.

You have got to visit the theme park because **we are** telling you that the new rollercoaster **is not** like normal rides. **It is** simply awesome. You **would not** believe it. I **could not** understand what all the fuss was about but **I will** tell you now – **you will** never have such an experience ever again.

_____

_____

_____

Time spent: _____ min _____ sec. Total: _____ out of 21   ©HarperCollins*Publishers* 2021

Date: _____

Day of week: _____

Tip *An apostrophe can be used to show that an object belongs to someone or something. This is known as possession. If the ball belongs to Kyle, the sentence could read, 'It is Kyle's ball.' The apostrophe followed by 's' after the name Kyle shows that the ball belongs to him.*

STEP 1 (1 min) Review

Circle the examples in which an **apostrophe** has been used correctly to show **possession**.

the dog's bone	lots of flower's	Rishi's pet hamster
Dads garden rose's	fish and chip's	the boat's mast

STEP 2 (2.5 min) Practise

Select and write correctly the word from each sentence which should have an **apostrophe** for **possession**.

We all stayed at Grandads house for the weekend. _____

Jack, who thinks plants are important, looks after his uncles shrubs. _____

I have many caps and some have the logo of the hats maker on them. _____

Although she writes for a newspaper, she is also the books author. _____

STEP 3 (1.5 min) Challenge

Rewrite the passage below, correcting errors in words using **apostrophes**.

We can't go to the shop's because my Gran's car has flat tyre's. We must borrow her neighbours pump and check if they have puncture's. If I can use Mums bike, I can go and get the pizza's from Adams take away.

_____

_____

_____

> **Tip**
>
> **Root words** are words which have meaning on their own such as *happy* and *possible*. The meaning of root words can be changed by adding **prefixes** and **suffixes**. Prefixes such as 'un-' and 'im-' can be added to the beginning of a root word: **un-** + happy = unhappy, im- + polite = impolite. Suffixes can be added to the end of words to change their meaning: polite + **ly** = politely, happy + **ly** = happily (with the 'y' at the end of happy changed to 'i').

STEP 1 (1 min) Review

Write the **root word** for each word.

sadness_____   undress _____   disagree _____

untidy _____   misbehave _____   dressed _____

STEP 2 (2.5 min) Practise

Match each **root word** to a suitable **prefix** or **suffix** then write the new word.

care	un-	_____
likely	mis-	_____
quick	-less	_____
place	-ly	_____

STEP 3 (1.5 min) Challenge

Put the words below into **two groups** according to their **roots**. There are **two words** that do not fit into either group. Write those words on the lines below.

| display | covering | discotheque | discover | unplayable |
| undiscoverable | uncovered | playfulness | plainly | playing |

_____   _____

STEP 1 (1 min) Review

- Add the correct word to each sentence.

The children had an _____ each.   **chocolate bar / sandwich / apple**

We went to Europe on a _____.   **boat / aeroplane / adventure**

The television was an _____ one.   **useless / modern / old**

I used a _____ jacket in the rain.   **orange / waterproof / umbrella**

STEP 2 (2.5 min) Practise

- Place a tick next to each sentence that is **correctly punctuated**.

They did not know how late it was.   ☐

How late they were going to bed!   ☐

"How late is it," asked Dan?   ☐

Dan asked, "How late is it?"   ☐

Were they late going to bed!   ☐

STEP 3 (1.5 min) Challenge

- Underline the words where an **apostrophe** is missing or incorrect. Write the correct spelling in the spaces below.

Theyl'l be late because Jacks car wont start. This always happens when wer'e in a rush. I'll need some help because Sues' bus is also running late. Youre never going to believe who else ca'nt get here on time. That's right – Mrs Smith, because her sons dog is poorly.

_____   _____   _____

_____   _____   _____

Date: _____

Day of week: _____

Tip *A prefix is a letter or letters added to the beginning of a word to change the meaning of that word.*

STEP 1 (1 min) **Review**

Underline the **prefix** in each word below and draw a line to match each word to its definition.

unkind   mishear   disagree

| not hear something correctly | have a different opinion | to be mean or not kind |

STEP 2 (2.5 min) **Practise**

Place a tick next to the correct words. Write the correct version next to the incorrect words.

disusual ☐ / _____   mistake ☐ / _____

unappear ☐ / _____   discover ☐ / _____

mishelpful ☐ / _____   untrust ☐ / _____

STEP 3 (1.5 min) **Challenge**

Underline the words with the incorrect **prefix**. Write the correct spelling in the spaces below.

There was a disunderstanding at lunchtime. It caused the most misimaginable fuss. Mr Smith and Miss Jones unagreed about which class should go to lunch first. Each was being rather misorganised which meant we all had to wait dishappily in the corridor. Miss Jones said her class was always first on Tuesdays but that is mistrue.

_____   _____   _____

_____   _____   _____

Time spent: _____ min _____ sec. Total: _____ out of 24

Date: _____

Day of week: _____

STEP 1 (1 min) Review

Underline the **prefix** and circle the **root** for each word.

inaccurate	irregular	undecided	impossible
distaste	illegal	immature	inactive

STEP 2 (2.5 min) Practise

Write each word below in the correct **prefix** column in the table.

accessible	perfect	regular	legal	mortal	patient
accurate	legible	responsible	adequate	relevant	logical

Prefix 'in-'	Prefix 'il-'	Prefix 'im-'	Prefix 'ir-'

STEP 3 (1.5 min) Challenge

Explain how the **prefixes** 'in-', 'im-' and 'il-' change the meaning of the **root word**.

_____

_____

Explain the meaning of **two** words from the table in Step 2.

_____

_____

Date: _____

Day of week: _____

Tip *Prefixes are often used to make new nouns and adjectives with different meanings than the original word.*

STEP 1 (1 min) Review

Write the **prefix** used in each of these words.

supermarket _____   international _____

impossible _____   disorganised _____

subheading _____   superstar _____

unintentional _____   invisible _____

STEP 2 (2.5 min) Practise

Match each **prefix** to the correct **root**, then write the new word.

inter-   septic   _____

auto-   marine   _____

anti-   city   _____

sub-   mobile   _____

STEP 3 (1.5 min) Challenge

Ensure each underlined **prefix** is matched to the correct word below and then write the words in the sentences.

| <u>anti</u>biography | <u>auto</u>way | <u>super</u>social | <u>sub</u>hero |

We got to the other side of the road through the _____.

The film was about a _____ who saved the world.

You were _____ at the party, ignoring everyone.

In her _____, she tells her life story.

Time spent: _____ min _____ sec. Total: _____ out of 16   ©HarperCollins*Publishers* 2021

Date: _____

Day of week: _____

Tip *The letter patterns 'ei', 'eigh' and 'ey' often make the long 'a' sound as represented by a–e in the words game, mane, late, wade and cape.*

STEP 1 (1 min) Review

Look at the words below. Write each word in the correct column in the table.

state	weigh	vein	sane	height	reign	rain
prey	play	freight	neighbour	their	holiday	grey

Long 'a' using 'ei'	Long 'a' using 'eigh'	Long 'a' using 'ey'	Other long 'a'	No long 'a'

STEP 2 (2.5 min) Practise

Complete the words below with the correct letters to represent the long '**a**' sound.

There were _____t people in the team – four boys and four girls.

They had to ob_____ the rules at school.

On the walk, they saw several r___ndeer.

The w_____t of their suitcases was checked at the airport.

STEP 3 (1.5 min) Challenge

Write **two** sentences containing words with the given long '**a**' sounds.

'ey' and 'eigh'

_____

'ei' and 'ai'

_____

Date: _____

Day of week: _____

> **Tip**
>
> *A suffix can be added to the end of a root word to change the meaning of the word. '-s' and '-es' are often used to change a noun from singular to plural, for example, cat → cats, fox → foxes. Other suffixes indicate changes in tense, for example, walk → walking, jump → jumped, or change words from one word class to another such as sad → sadness, quiet → quietly. Sometimes the suffix is added without any change to the spelling of the root word, but sometimes changes are made to the root: happy → happiness, run → running, baby → babies.*

STEP 1 (1 min) Review

Write the **root word** for the words in bold in each sentence.

The fireworks made an **incredibly** loud noise. _____

There was much **merriment** at the wedding. _____

We marvelled at the fantastic **climbing** skills of the squirrel. _____

She got many **replies** to her request for volunteers. _____

STEP 2 (2.5 min) Practise

Complete the passage below. Use the given **root words** and add a suitable **suffix** to each. Ensure each word is in the correct position so that the passage makes sense.

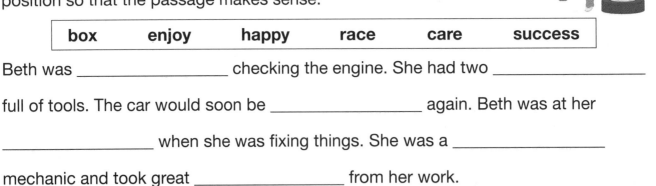

box	enjoy	happy	race	care	success

Beth was _____ checking the engine. She had two _____

full of tools. The car would soon be _____ again. Beth was at her

_____ when she was fixing things. She was a _____

mechanic and took great _____ from her work.

STEP 3 (1.5 min) Challenge

Explain what happens to the spelling of each word below when the given **suffix** is added:

when adding '**-ness**' to '**silly**'.

_____

when adding '**-ing**' to '**hike**'.

_____

Time spent: _____ min _____ sec. Total: _____ out of 12

Date: _____

Day of week: _____

Tip *If the final syllable of a word is stressed and that word ends in one consonant letter with just one vowel before it, the final consonant is doubled before adding any **suffix** beginning with a vowel. For example, begin → beginning, forget → forgetting.*

STEP 1 (1 min) Review

Add the words below to the correct column in the table and write each **root word**.

| jumping | running | tapping | gardening | beginner | rapidly |

Final letter doubled before adding suffix	Root word	Suffix added with no change to root word	Root word

STEP 2 (2.5 min) Practise

Correct the spelling of each word in bold in the text below.

Emma's cat was growing **fater** each day. When her mum **noticced** she

[   ]   [   ]

quickkly realised that the cat **prefered** to eat the dog's food. No

[   ]   [   ]

wonder the dog was **geting** much, much **thiner**.

[   ]   [   ]

STEP 3 (1.5 min) Challenge

Write each sentence again, ensuring the **root word** in bold is given the **correct suffix**.

Each family was **limit** to buying four tickets for the school play.

_____

Mum was **refer** to Sally when she talked about being helpful.

_____

27 Suffixes (3)

Date: _____

Day of week: _____

Tip The suffix '-ly' turns adjectives into adverbs. Some nouns are also turned into adverbs or adjectives with the addition of '-ly'.

STEP 1 (1 min) Review

Decide whether the word in bold in each sentence is correct by placing a tick or a cross in the box. For incorrect words, write the correct version.

The snail moved very **slow** across the path. ☐ _____

It was **love** that they could play together so well. ☐ _____

James had to go **directly** to the school office. ☐ _____

She tiptoed **silent** through the garden. ☐ _____

STEP 2 (2.5 min) Practise

Add the **suffix '-ly'** to each word below and add the new word to the correct sentence. At the end of each sentence, state the **word class** (noun, verb, adjective or adverb) of the word you have added.

unkind	urgent	expert	friend	slight

You will meet my very _____ cousins at the party. _____

Jack is only _____ taller than Ella. _____

They needed an ambulance _____. _____

Dad _____ placed the candles on the cake. _____

_____, she pushed the boy into the pool. _____

STEP 3 (1.5 min) Challenge

Rewrite each sentence below, changing the word / words in bold by adding the **suffix '-ly'**.

≡ NEWS ≡

We will be there in a **short** amount of time.

_____

We have the newspaper delivered **every week**.

_____

Time spent: _____ min _____ sec. Total: _____ out of 19

Date: _____

Day of week: _____

Tip Not all additions of the **suffix '-ly'** are straightforward. Sometimes, the end of the root word needs to be removed or amended when adding the **suffix '-ly'**. For example, happy → happily, gentle → gently, basic → basically.

STEP 1 (1 min) Review

Add the adverbs below to the correct column in the table and write each **root word**.

basically	smoothly	merrily	actually	angrily	historically

Only '-ly' added to root word	Root word	Ending with '-ily'	Root word	Ending with '-ally'	Root word

STEP 2 (2.5 min) Practise

Add the correct **suffix** to each word to make an adverb. Use a dictionary to help if you are unsure.

crazy   _____   dramatic   _____

terrible   _____   lucky   _____

frantic   _____   simple   _____

STEP 3 (1.5 min) Challenge

Write a rule for adding the **suffix '-ly'** to:

words ending in '**-ic**' such as '**phonetic**' and '**basic**'.

_____

words ending in '**-le**' such as '**humble**' and '**noble**'.

_____

Date: _____

Day of week: _____

Tip Adding the suffix '-ous' to a noun changes it into an *adjective*. For example, *danger → dangerous*. Sometimes the ending of the root word changes before adding '-ous' as in *vary → various*.

STEP 1 (1 min) Review

Add the **suffix** '-ous' to each **root word** below.

poison_____

mountain_____

murder_____

joy_____

STEP 2 (2.5 min) Practise

The **root word** for each of the words below has had changes made to it before adding the **suffix** '-ous'. Write each word in the correct column and in the next column write the root word.

glorious	nervous	humorous	envious	glamorous	famous

'y' ending changed to 'i' before adding '-ous'	Root word	'e' ending dropped before adding '-ous'	Root word	'u' removed from 'our' ending before adding '-ous'	Root word

STEP 3 (1.5 min) Challenge

Words such as '**adventure**' and '**virtue**' end in '**e**' which is dropped before adding '**-ous**'. The words below keep their '**e**' ending when adding '**-ous**'. What do you notice about these words?

advantageous	courageous	outrageous

_____

_____

Time spent: _____ min _____ sec. Total: _____ out of 17

©HarperCollins*Publishers* 2021

STEP 1 (1 min) **Review**

- Add the correct **prefix 'in-', 'il-', 'im-'** or **'ir-'** to each **root word**.

visible _____   relevant _____   rational _____

polite _____   correct _____   logical _____

STEP 2 (2.5 min) **Practise**

- Correct the spelling of each word in bold in the text below.

We had to **way** the fruit before we **peid** for it. It was then a long walk home in the

[_____]   [_____]

rane so we could deliver it to our **naybour** who lives at number **ate**. She said we

[_____]   [_____]   [_____]

looked like a **freyght** train carrying so many bags.

[_____]

STEP 3 (1.5 min) **Challenge**

- Rewrite each sentence below, changing the words in bold into **adverbs** using the **suffix '-ly'**.

They knew they should go **direct** home but something had moved **quick** in the woods.

_____

Lucky, it was still not **proper** dark so they went to look, despite Raj acting a bit **dramatic**.

_____

_____

They all crept along **silent**, and Raj seemed to be **actual** enjoying himself.

_____

Noble, he pushed some nettles aside so the others would not get stung.

_____

31 Word families

Date: _____

Day of week: _____

Tip *Word families have a common root word or a common spelling pattern.*

STEP 1 (1 min) Review

What do the words in each set of words have in common?

elephant, alphabet, telephone

_____

kindness, unkind, kindly

_____

STEP 2 (2.5 min) Practise

Sort the words below into **three** different **word families**.

nervously	event	valiantly	uneventful	valour	nerves
	unnerving	eventually	valiant		

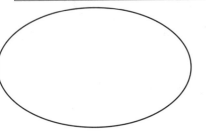 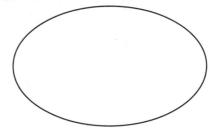 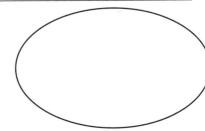

STEP 3 (1.5 min) Challenge

Write a sentence for each of the words below. Show an understanding of the differences in meaning of each word.

sense _____

sensible _____

sensitive _____

34   Time spent: _____ min _____ sec. Total: _____ out of 14   ©HarperCollins*Publishers* 2021

Date: _____

Day of week: _____

Tip The letters 'ou' are used together in many words, making different sounds. Sometimes they make the short 'u' sound as in 'hut' and 'push'.

STEP 1 (1 min) Review

Read each word below. Underline the words with a short 'u' sound spelled 'ou'.

jump   country   count   nourish   round   courageous   county   huff

STEP 2 (2.5 min) Practise

Place a tick or a cross in the box next to each word to show whether the correct spelling has been used for the short 'u' sound. Where the spelling is incorrect, write the correct spelling for the word.

dubble ☐ _____   stouble ☐ _____   lunch ☐ _____

rubble ☐ _____   truble ☐ _____   cusin ☐ _____

noutty ☐ _____   rugh ☐ _____   young ☐ _____

STEP 3 (1.5 min) Challenge

Complete each word using the clues to help.

f l __ __ __ i s h   When something grows or develops healthily.

e n c __ __ __ a g e   Support or give confidence to someone.

t __ __ __ h   One of our senses.

c __ __ p l __   Two of something.

Tip *Some words contain letters which are not sounded when the word is spoken. For example: 'write' – silent 'w', 'gnat' – silent 'g', 'scent' – silent 'c'.*

STEP 1 (1 min) Review

Read the words below. Next to each, write the letter(s) not pronounced.

gnome   ____   thumb   ____   isle   ____

written   ____   Wednesday   ____   dough   ____

STEP 2 (2.5 min) Practise

Choose the correct word to fit in each space in the passage below.

| doubt | aisle | wrapped | knight | night |

The happy couple walked down the _____ of the

church. They then _____ their arms around each other. From the

first _____ that they met, she had no _____ that she

would save the _____ from the dragon and marry him.

STEP 3 (1.5 min) Challenge

Use the clues below to help you write the correct words with unpronounced letters.

A baby sheep.   _____ (unpronounced 'b')

A piece of land surrounded by water.   _____ (unpronounced 's')

A word used if something is incorrect.   _____ (unpronounced 'w')

Closing buttons or a zip.   _____ (unpronounced 't')

Time spent: _____ min _____ sec. Total: _____ out of 15

Tip   *The spelling pattern 'ough' appears in many words and represents a number of different sounds.*

STEP 1 (1 min) Review

Underline the words with the same long 'o' sound as represented by 'o' in the word 'no'.

row   though   sew   through   trough   tough   groan

Underline the words with same 'oo' sound as represented by 'oo' in the word 'too'.

flew   bough   thorough   thought   blue   grew

STEP 2 (2.5 min) Practise

Write **three** words which rhyme with each of the words below.

rough   _____   _____   _____

bough   _____   _____   _____

nought   _____   _____   _____

though   _____   _____   _____

STEP 3 (1.5 min) Challenge

Write a sentence for each given word. Use a dictionary to help you.

ought _____

thorough _____

drought _____

Tricky words ('ear' words)

Date: _____

Day of week: _____

Tip *The spelling pattern 'ear' is used to represent different sounds.*

STEP 1 (1 min) Review

Match each word on the left with a word it rhymes with from the right. Add **one** more rhyming word for each.

ear	bird	_____
learn	weird	_____
heard	cart	_____
heart	burn	_____

STEP 2 (2.5 min) Practise

Complete the passage by using the correct form of the words containing the 'ear' spelling.

We waited all night for the ghost to **appeer** _____. At one point, we

thought we **hurd** _____ a strange sound and our

harts _____ started to beat quickly. We soon **lurned** _____

that it was a tree tapping against the side of the shed. In the **errly** _____

morning light, my **deer** _____ friend Josie said she saw something

move across the garden but it was just the cat.

STEP 3 (1.5 min) Challenge

Explain the different sound made by the spelling pattern 'ear' in the words '**fear**', '**earth**' and '**bear**' by giving examples of words they rhyme with, for example, fear → beer.

_____

_____

_____

Time spent: _____ min _____ sec. Total: _____ out of 17

©HarperCollins*Publishers* 2021

Spelling from the Greek language

Tip *The 'ch' spelling pattern in words of **Greek origin** sounds like the sound represented by 'k' in kid.*

STEP 1 (1 min) Review

Match each definition to the correct word.

Sound reflected back from a surface   orchid

A type of flower   chorus

An important organ in the body   echo

Part of a song   stomach

STEP 2 (2.5 min) Practise

Choose a word from below that uses '**ch**' to make the '**k**' sound to complete each sentence.

architect	monarch	chorus	character

Jack is the main _____ in a story about a boy and a beanstalk.

A _____ is the king or queen of a country.

Buildings are designed by an _____.

We all joined in with the _____ of the song.

STEP 3 (1.5 min) Challenge

Write a definition for each word below. Use a dictionary to help you.

anchor _____

mechanic _____

orchestra _____

Date: _____

Day of week: _____

Tip | *The 'ch' spelling pattern in words of **French origin** sounds like the 'sh' sound made by the letters 'sh' in words such as 'shop'. Words which use the 'ch' to make this sound have to be learned to avoid confusion.*

STEP 1 (1 min) Review

Place a tick next to each word in which 'ch' makes a 'sh' sound.

school ☐   chef ☐   chute ☐   chop ☐   munching ☐

crochet ☐   change ☐   attach ☐   chorus ☐   champagne ☐

STEP 2 (2.5 min) Practise

Match each phrase to its related 'ch' word. Use a dictionary if you are unsure.

An ornate light   machine

A type of food made from egg   brochure

A piece of equipment   chandelier

A large and stately house   chateau

A booklet often containing information or products for sale quiche

STEP 3 (1.5 min) Challenge

Read each clue and complete the words containing 'ch'. Use a dictionary if you are unsure.

p a r a _ _ _ _ _ _   Needed if jumping out of an aeroplane.

c _ _ a u f f e u r   A person who drives others around.

c _ _ a l e t   A small house often used for holidays.

m o u s t a _ _ _ _   Facial hair between the nose and upper lip.

Time spent: _____ min _____ sec. Total: _____ out of 13   ©HarperCollins*Publishers* 2021

Date: _____

Day of week: _____

Tip *Homophones* are words which sound exactly the same when spoken but have a different spelling and meaning. It is important to know the correct spelling and meaning of homophones to avoid confusion.

STEP 1 (1 min) Review

Circle the correct **homophone** in each sentence.

They were happy to be attending the **bawl / ball**.

They could not see **through / threw** the dirty window.

The **knot / not** was difficult to untie.

Sam gave a **grown / groan** when mum told him to tidy his bedroom.

STEP 2 (2.5 min) Practise

Write a sentence for each **homophone**.

allowed _____

aloud _____

plain _____

plane _____

STEP 3 (1.5 min) Challenge

Explain the difference between each pair of **homophones**.

their and **there** _____

_____

here and **hear** _____

_____

Time spent: _____ min _____ sec. Total: _____ out of 10

Date: _____

Day of week: _____

Tip *A near-homophone sounds almost the same as another word.*

STEP 1 (1 min) Review

Write a sentence for each given word.

quiet _____

quite _____

one _____

won _____

STEP 2 (2.5 min) Practise

Underline the **two** pairs (**four** words) of **near-homophones** in the sentence below.

We'll all accept your invitation except for George because the wheel fell off his car.

Write a short sentence for each word you have underlined above.

_____

_____

_____

_____

STEP 3 (1.5 min) Challenge

Explain the difference between the **homophones** 'he'll', 'heal' and 'heel'.

_____

_____

Time spent: _____ min _____ sec. Total: _____ out of 15

STEP 1 (1 min) Review

- Read the text below. Underline the words which contain letters that are not pronounced.

Last Wednesday, I went to feed the lambs when I trapped my thumb in the barn

door. Gran wrapped it in a wet cloth but that night it really throbbed. A few days

later I knew it was broken so I went to the hospital.

STEP 2 (2.5 min) Practise

- Add the 'ou' spelling to each word below to make the 'u' sound as in 'cup'. Then fill in the gaps in the passage using the correct completed words.

d____ble   y____nger   t____ch   tr____ble   c____sin   c____rage

There was definitely _____ ahead. My _____ had been round to

visit and had shown _____ rescuing my _____ sister. She was there

at the _____ when my sister tried to _____ a fish and fell into the pond.

STEP 3 (1.5 min) Challenge

- Each sentence below contains incorrect **homophones** in bold. Write the **correct homophones** in the spaces provided beneath each sentence.

Their is definitely a garage near **hear**, he thought as the car stopped.

_____   _____

Nobody **new** how old the kittens were but they had certainly **groan**.

_____   _____

It was **plane** to **sea** that they were not **aloud** to play there.

_____   _____   _____

ANSWERS

Test 1
Step 1:
loud; fast
slow; tall
Step 2:
Each sentence to have a suitable match and have appropriate **adjectives** added for each given **noun**. Examples:
Sam was running ———— on the **wet, muddy** field.
Dad paid ———— the **kind, helpful** taxi driver.
Martha looked at ———— the **beautiful, detailed** painting.
Brewster barked at ———— the **big, ginger** cat.
Step 3:
Each **sentence** to relate to the picture and contain an **expanded noun phrase**. Examples:
The child flew **the pretty, colourful kite**.
Lucy splashed in **the warm, blue sea**.

Test 2
Step 1:
Variations are acceptable but each sentence must make sense.
Examples: slowly; carefully; greedily; silently.
Step 2:
Accept spelling errors but discuss the way in which the word endings change.
happily, amazing
incredibly, huge
wearily, cosy
Step 3:
Adjectives – <u>amazing</u>, <u>huge</u>, <u>red</u>, <u>scary</u>, <u>silly</u>, <u>mighty</u>
Adverbs – (rapidly), (restlessly), (angrily), (slowly), (quickly)

Test 3
Step 1:
Variations are acceptable but each sentence must make sense.
Examples: but; when / because; because / when; or.
Step 2:
Each sentence to use a suitable **conjunction**. Examples:
They had ice cold water **because** they were hot.
It was a long journey **and** the car was uncomfortable.
Step 3:
and, C
if, S
or, C

Test 4
Step 1:
because; so; if; when
Step 2:
Java eats lots of fruit because it is healthy. ✓
Nature will water the garden if it rains. ✓
Step 3:
Accept variations in wording but ensure the correct **conjunction** is used. Examples:
The snow in the garden will melt **because / if** it is a warm day.
The twins were excited **because** it was their birthday.
We can go outside **if** we finish our lunch. / We can go outside **because** we finished our lunch.

Test 5
Step 1:
after; before; while; when

Step 2:
They were all throwing snowballs **before** ———— their hands got so cold.
We could not use the car **after** ———— it broke down.
Lucy was asleep **while** ———— the thunderstorm raged. (Also accept **before**.)
They always go camping **when** ———— it is the summer holidays. (Also accept **while**.)
Step 3:
Accept correctly formed and appropriate sentences using the given **conjunction**. Examples:
We got very cold **before** we had a hot drink.
The children built a snowman **when** it snowed.

Test 6
Step 1:
since; through; therefore; soon
Step 2:
Example answers (there are other possibilities): eventually – time; otherwise – cause; everywhere – place.
Step 3:
Each sentence must be correctly punctuated and use the given **adverb** appropriately. Examples:
They ate their meal and went for a walk **afterwards**.
Ella worked hard and **consequently** got lots of house points.

Test 7
Step 1:
next (to), P; in, P; after, T; on, P
Step 2:
Each sentence should make sense with a correct **preposition** used for place or time. Examples:
The dog jumped **over** the fence.
Later, he was given a medal.
Step 3:
They had PE **on** Monday. They all loved being **in** the school gym. They had to walk **through** the playground to get there. There was always time for a game **during** the lesson.

Test 8
Step 1:
ate; flew; played; kicked
Step 2:
<u>were flying</u> – past; <u>are swimming</u> – present; <u>is blowing</u> – present; <u>was purring</u> – past
Step 3:
were leading; was standing; was thinking

Test 9
Step 1:
have; has; has; have
Step 2:
Ensure the correct form of **to have** and the **past participle** of the main verb is used:
They **have performed** in a talent show.
Emile **has completed** all his homework.
My sister **has walked** to school.
The teachers **have talked** to us about being kind.
Step 3:
The explanation should acknowledge that the verb 'to have' has not been used in its correct form (change to **have**) and the **past participle** of the verb 'to race' has not been used (change to **raced**).

Test 10: Progress Test 1

Step 1:

Conjunctions showing cause	Conjunctions showing time
so	when
because	after
if	while

Step 2:
during / throughout; on / over; under / in; before

Step 3:
The children **were running** in a race.
Everyone **played** in the stream before they **walked** home.
The whole class **has walked** to the swimming baths.

Test 11

Step 1:
a; an; an; a

Step 2:
If the **adjective** follows 'an', it must start with a vowel and if it follows 'a' it must start with a consonant. Accept suitable answers.
Examples:
From the mountain top, they could see an **amazing / awesome** view.
All the children wanted to play on an **old / ancient** swing in the garden.
The birthday cake was in the shape of a **red / blue / fast** car.
Everybody laughed when she told a **funny / hilarious / good** joke.

Step 3:
We had <u>an</u> early lunch and went on <u>an</u> adventure in <u>a</u> big boat.
A huge whale passed by and we saw <u>an</u> octopus and an old shipwreck.
'a apple' is incorrect because apple begins with a vowel sound
'an melon' is incorrect because an is only used before a vowel sound

Test 12

Step 1:
Edward, **I**taly, **T**uesday, **J**upiter, **A**pril, **L**ucy

Step 2:
Every **W**ednesday during the month of **F**ebruary, **M**rs **J**ones will swim with crocodiles in the **R**iver **N**ile near the city of **C**airo in **E**gypt.

Step 3:
Explanation should acknowledge that 'ocean' and 'river' are **nouns / common nouns** identifying generic places, but 'River Thames' and 'Pacific Ocean' are **proper nouns** naming these particular places.
Explanation should identify that with a **capital letter** 'March' refers to the month, but without it refers to 'marching'. (Also accept that it could refer to a named 'march' with a capital letter, e.g. the Greenpeace Protest March.)

Test 13

Step 1:
It was a lovely day when Harry went surfing. ✓

Step 2:
Explanation should acknowledge that the sentence neither starts with a **capital letter** nor ends with a **full stop**.

Step 3:
The divers were fascinated by the shark**.** **I**t was gliding silently through the water like a sleek, grey submarine beneath their boat**.** **W**hen it was close enough, **M**artha took a photograph**.**

Test 14

Step 1:
What an incredible view we saw! ✓
Is it time to leave? ✓

Step 2:
What a huge beanstalk Jack saw before him!
Where could it have come from**?**
How would he climb it**?**
How terrifying the giant was!

Step 3:
During the day, the creature sleeps but at night it stirs in its cave**.** It sees well in the dark as it creeps through the forest**.** Munch! It snatches a small mammal from a tree branch! What could it be**?** What else does it eat**?** How incredible this creature is!

Test 15

Step 1:
We saw elephants**,** lions**,** giraffes and baboons when we went to the zoo.
They visited the cities of London**,** Manchester**,** Birmingham and Leeds on their holiday.
(For both responses above, also accept a comma before 'and' (the serial or Oxford comma). This is not specifically taught in most schools but is also correct.)

Step 2:
Hetty could play the guitar, the violin, the cello and the piano. ✓

Step 3:
Accept any sentences which **make sense** and **punctuate lists** correctly. (Also accept a comma before 'and' – see note in Step 1.)
Examples:
At the supermarket, Dad bought cheese, bread, crisps and coffee.
Mum would like to swim, surf, sunbathe and read at the beach.

Test 16

Step 1:
<u>Go and get your uniform on</u> said Mum.
<u>This is the best food I've ever tasted</u> said Jack.
Dad asked <u>is this the correct train for York?</u>
<u>What fantastic acting that was</u> exclaimed Cally.

Step 2:
"It's absolutely freezing!" screamed Netty. ✓
Gran said, "I think you were tricked, Netty." ✓

Step 3:
"Shark! Shark!" yelled Dan.
Gran shouted, "Get out of the water! Quick!"
"It's ok Gran," laughed Netty.
"Dan has a dog called Shark," explained Alex.

Test 17

Step 1:
I am —— I'm; you are —— you're; he is —— he's; could not —— couldn't; will not —— won't; did not —— didn't

Step 2:
We're —— We are; It'll —— It will; don't —— do not; haven't —— have not; they'll —— they will; they're —— they are; she's —— she is

Step 3:
You've got to visit the theme park because **we're** telling you that the new rollercoaster **isn't** like normal rides. **It's** simply awesome. You **wouldn't** believe it. I **couldn't** understand what all the fuss was about but **I'll** tell you now – **you'll** never have such an experience ever again.

Test 18

Step 1:
the dog's bone   Rishi's pet hamster   the boat's mast

Step 2:
Grandad's; uncle's; hat's; book's

Step 3:
We can't go to the **shops** because my Gran's car has flat **tyres**. We must borrow her **neighbour's / neighbours'** pump and check if they have **punctures**. If I can use **Mum's** bike, I can go and get the **pizzas** from **Adam's** take away.

Test 19

Step 1:
sad; dress; agree
tidy; behave; dress

Step 2:
careless; unlikely; quickly; misplace

Step 3:
First circle: display; unplayable; playfulness; playing
Second circle: covering; discover; undiscoverable; uncovered
Two words: discotheque; plainly

Test 20: Progress Test 2

Step 1:
The children had an **apple** each.
We went to Europe on a **boat**.
The television was an **old** one.
I used a **waterproof** jacket in the rain.

Step 2:
They did not know how late it was. ✓
How late they were going to bed! ✓
Dan asked, "How late is it?" ✓

Step 3:
Theyl'l be late because Jacks car wont start. This always happens when wer'e in a rush. I'll need some help because Sues' bus is also running late. Youre never going to believe who else ca'nt get here on time. That's right – Mrs Smith, because her sons dog is poorly.
They'll; Jack's; won't; we're; Sue's; You're; can't; son's

Test 21

Step 1:
unkind ——— to be mean or not kind
mishear ——— not hear something correctly
disagree ——— have a different opinion

Step 2:
disusual – unusual; mistake ✓; unappear – disappear; discover ✓; mishelpful – unhelpful; untrust – mistrust

Step 3:
There was a disunderstanding at lunchtime. It caused the most misimaginable fuss. Mr Smith and Miss Jones unagreed about which class should go to lunch first. Each was being rather misorganised which meant we all had to wait dishappily in the corridor. Miss Jones said her class was always first on Tuesdays but that is mistrue.
misunderstanding; unimaginable; disagreed; disorganised; unhappily; untrue

Test 22

Step 1:
in(accurate)   ir(regular)   un(decided)   im(possible)
di(staste)   il(legal)   im(mature)   in(active)

Step 2:

Prefix 'in-'	Prefix 'il-'	Prefix 'im-'	Prefix 'ir-'
accessible	legal	mortal	relevant
accurate	legible	patient	responsible
adequate	logical	perfect	regular

Step 3:
The explanation should acknowledge that these prefixes give an opposite or negative meaning to the words.

The explanation should state that the prefixes give the opposite or negative meaning, and two words should be correctly defined.

Test 23

Step 1:
super   inter
im   dis
sub   super
un   in

Step 2:
inter- ——— city, intercity
auto- ——— mobile, automobile
anti- ——— septic, antiseptic
sub- ——— marine, submarine

Step 3:
We got to the other side of the road through the subway.
The film was about a superhero who saved the world.
You were antisocial at the party, ignoring everyone.
In her autobiography, she tells her life story.

Test 24

Step 1:

Long 'a' using 'ei'	Long 'a' using 'eigh'	Long 'a' using 'ey'	Other long 'a'	No long 'a'
vein	weigh	prey	state	height
reign	freight	grey	sane	their
	neighbour		rain	
			play	
			holiday	

Step 2:
There were **eigh**t people in the team – four boys and four girls.
They had to ob**ey** the rules at school.
On the walk, they saw several r**ei**ndeer.
The w**eigh**t of their suitcases was checked at the airport.

Step 3:
Each sentence must be correctly punctuated and use the given spelling patterns appropriately. Example answers:
The fr**eigh**t was carried on a large, gr**ey** ship.
The bride's **veil** got wet in the **rain**.

Test 25

Step 1:
incredible; merry; climb; reply

Step 2:
Beth was carefully checking the engine. She had two boxes full of tools. The car would soon be racing again. Beth was at her happiest when she was fixing things. She was a successful mechanic and took great enjoyment from her work.

Step 3:
Explanation should contain the key information shown in the examples below:
silliness – exchange the **y** for an **i** then add '-**ness**'
hiking – remove the **e** then add '-**ing**'

Test 26

Step 1:

Final letter doubled before adding suffix	Root word	Suffix added with no change to root word	Root word
running	run	jumping	jump
tapping	tap	gardening	garden
beginner	begin	rapidly	rapid

Step 2:
fatter; noticed
quickly; preferred
getting; thinner
Step 3:
limited
referring

Test 27
Step 1:
×, slowly
×, lovely
✓
×, silently
Step 2:

You will meet my very <u>friendly</u> cousins at the party.	adjective
Jack is only <u>slightly</u> taller than Ella.	adverb
They needed an ambulance <u>urgently</u>.	adverb
Dad <u>expertly</u> placed the candles on the cake.	adverb
<u>Unkindly</u>, she pushed the boy into the pool.	adverb

Step 3:
Example sentences (ensure 'shortly' and 'weekly' are used correctly):
We will be there **shortly**.
Weekly, we have the newspaper delivered.

Test 28
Step 1:

Only '-ly' added to root word	Root word	Ending with '-ily'	Root word	Ending with '-ally'	Root word
smoothly actually	smooth actual	merrily angrily	merry angry	basically historically	basic historic

Step 2:
crazily; dramatically
terribly; luckily
frantically; simply
Step 3:
Each explanation should be similar to the examples below:
If the root word ends in '-ic', '-ally' is (usually) added.
If the root word ends in '-le', the 'le' is changed to '-ly'.

Test 29
Step 1:
poison**ous**; mountain**ous**
murder**ous**; joy**ous**
Step 2:

'y' ending changed to 'i' before adding '-ous'	Root word	'e' ending dropped before adding '-ous'	Root word	'u' removed from 'our' ending before adding '-ous'	Root word
glorious envious	glory envy	nervous famous	nerve fame	humorous glamorous	humour glamour

Step 3:
Explanation should acknowledge that each of these words has a (soft) **g** sound at the end of the root word which is kept in the **root word + '-ous'**.

Test 30: Progress Test 3
Step 1:
invisible; **ir**relevant; **ir**rational
impolite; **in**correct; **il**logical
Step 2:
We had to **weigh** the fruit before we **paid** for it. It was then a long walk home in the **rain** so we could deliver it to our **neighbour** who lives at number **eight**. She said we looked like a **freight** train carrying so many bags.
Step 3:
direct**ly**, quick**ly**;
Luck**i**ly, proper**ly**, dramatical**ly**;
silent**ly**, actual**ly**;
nob**ly**

Test 31
Step 1:
Each includes the spelling **ph** representing the **f** sound.
Each has the root word 'kind'.
Step 2:
nervously, nerves, unnerving
event, uneventful, eventually
valiantly, valour, valiant
Step 3:
Each response should demonstrate an understanding of the given word. Examples:
The dog used its **sense** of smell to find the bone.
We were all **sensible** on the school trip.
Some plants are very **sensitive** to the cold.

Test 32
Step 1:
<u>c</u>ountry, <u>n</u>ourish, <u>c</u>ourag<u>eou</u>s
Step 2:
× double; × stubble; ✓
✓; × trouble; × cousin
× nutty; × rough; ✓
Step 3:
fl<u>our</u>ish; enc<u>our</u>age; t<u>ou</u>ch; c<u>ou</u>ple

Test 33
Step 1:
gnome g; thum**b** b; isl**e** s
written w; Wednes**d**ay d; do**ugh** ugh
Step 2:
The happy couple walked down the **aisle** of the church. They then **wrapped** their arms around each other. From the first **night** that they met, she had no **doubt** that she would save the **knight** from the dragon and marry him.
Step 3:
lam**b**; is**land** / i**sle**; **w**rong; fa**s**ten

Test 34
Step 1:
<u>row</u>, <u>though</u>, <u>sew</u>, <u>groan</u>
<u>flew</u>, <u>blue</u>, <u>grew</u>
Step 2:
Ensure words chosen rhyme with the given word. Examples:
rough – tough, stuff, huff
bough – cow, row, now
nought – taught, sport, caught, sort, bought, fought, thought
though – row, low, show, although

Step 3:
Ensure sentences use the given words correctly.
Examples:
We **ought** to try camping in the summer.
They gave the house a **thorough** cleaning.
The lack of rain led to a long **drought**.

Test 35

Step 1:
ear ——— weird, e.g. fear
learn ——— burn, e.g. turn
heard ——— bird, e.g. word
heart ——— cart, e.g. dart

Step 2:
We waited all night for the ghost to **appear**. At one point we thought we **heard** a strange sound and our **hearts** started to beat quickly. We soon **learned** that it was a tree tapping against the side of the shed. In the **early** morning light, my **dear** friend Josie said she saw something move across the garden but it was just the cat.

Step 3:
The explanation should acknowledge that:
In fear the '**ear**' sound is like in the word ear. In earth it sounds like the '**er**' sound in bird and in bear it sounds like '**air**' (different example words may be used).

Test 36

Step 1:
Sound reflected back from a surface ——— echo
A type of flower ——— orchid
An important organ in the body ——— stomach
Part of a song ——— chorus

Step 2:
Jack is the main **character** in a story about a boy and a beanstalk.
A **monarch** is the king or queen of a country.
Buildings are designed by an **architect**.
We all joined in with the **chorus** of the song.

Step 3:
anchor – a metal tool used to prevent ships drifting at sea
mechanic – a person who builds or repairs machines
orchestra – a group of musicians playing instruments together

Test 37

Step 1:
chef ✓   chute ✓
crochet ✓   champagne ✓

Step 2:
An ornate light ——— chandelier
A type of food made from egg ——— quiche
A piece of equipment ——— machine
A large and stately house ——— chateau
A booklet often containing information or products
for sale ——— brochure

Step 3:
para**chute**
chauffeur
chalet
mousta**che**

Test 38

Step 1:
They were happy to be attending the bawl / (ball).
They could not see (through) / threw the dirty window.
The (knot) / not was difficult to untie.
Sam gave a grown / (groan) when mum told him to tidy his bedroom.

Step 2:
Each sentence must use the given word correctly. Examples:
We are not **allowed** to play on the grass.
I read my story **aloud** to the class.
The **plain** paper was ready for her to draw on.
We flew to Greece in a **plane**.

Step 3:
Each explanation must make sense. Examples:
'Their' means belonging to someone and 'there' refers to a place.
'Here' refers to a place and 'hear' means to notice sounds.

Test 39

Step 1:
Each sentence must make sense. Examples:
It was **quiet** in the library.
I **quite** like that film.
Priya has **one** brother.
Archie **won** the prize.

Step 2:
We'll all accept your invitation except for George because the wheel fell off his car.
Example sentences:
We'll see you tomorrow.
I can't accept that behaviour.
Everyone has chips except Jack who has salad.
The wheel of the bus is huge.

Step 3:
Explanation should make the differences clear. Examples:
'He'll' is the contracted form of 'he will'.
'Heal' means to get or make better.
'Heel' is the back part of the foot.

Test 40: Progress Test 4

Step 1:
Last Wednesday, I went to feed the lambs when I trapped my thumb in the barn door. Gran wrapped it in a wet cloth but that night it really throbbed. A few days later I knew it was broken so I went to the hospital.

Step 2:
There was definitely trouble ahead. My cousin had been round to visit and had shown courage rescuing my younger sister. She was there at the double when my sister tried to touch a fish and fell into the pond.

Step 3:
There; here
knew; grown
plain; see; allowed